Behavior in Living Things

Michael Bright

Chicago, Illinois

www.capstonepub.com
Visit our website to find out more information about Heinemann-Raintree books.

To order:
☎ Phone 888-454-2279
💻 Visit www.capstonepub.com
to browse our catalog and order online.

Edited by Andrew Farrow, Adrian Vigliano, and Diyan Leake
Designed by Victoria Allen
Picture research by Elizabeth Alexander
Original illustrations © Capstone Global Library Ltd 2012
Illustrations by Oxford Designers & Illustrators
Originated by Capstone Global Library Ltd
Printed and bound in the United States by Corporate Graphics

15 14 13 12 11
10 9 8 7 6 5 4 3 2 1

Library of Congress Cataloging-in-Publication Data
Cataloging-in-Publication data is on file at the Library of Congress.

ISBN: 978-1-4109-4425-2 (HC) 978-1-4109-4432-0 (PB)

Acknowledgments
The author and publishers are grateful to the following for permission to reproduce copyright material: Behavioural Ecology Research Group, Oxford University p. 17; Corbis p. 14 bottom (© Norbert Wu/Science Faction); Ewa Krzyszczyk/Dolphins of Shark Bay Project p. 30); FLPA pp. 12 (© Cyril Ruoso/Minden Pictures); 25 (© Jim Brandenburg/Minden Pictures); 27 (© Frans Lanting; iStockphoto pp. 24 (© Andy Gehrig); 35 top (© Sharon Dominick); 36 (© Sandeep Subba); Nature Picture Library p. 31 (© Miles Barton); NHPA pp. 8 (Andy Rouse); 15 (Phil Degginger); Photolibrary pp. 4 (Watt Jim); 6 (Splashdown Direct); 16 (Michel Gunther); 18 (Fritz Polking); 20 (Cyril Ruoso); 23 (Konrad Wothe); 29 (BIOS); 28 bottom right (Clive Bromhall); 28 left (Corbis); 40 (AlaskaStock); 41 (Janine Wiedel); Reuters p. 11 (STR New); Science Photo Library p. 38 (BSIP Astier); Shutterstock pp. 5 (© Monkey Business Images); 9 (© Mogens Trolle); 10 (© Peter Kirillov); 13 (© Neale Cousland); 14 top (© Image Focus); 19 (© Pang Chee Seng Philip); 21 (© cbpix); 22 (© János Németh); 28 top right (© Ronald van der Beek); 33 (© Cathy Keifer); 35 bottom (© Elena Elisseeva); 37 (© Graeme Dawes); 39 (© Creatista).

Cover photograph of a springbok pronking in Kruger National Park, South Africa, reproduced with permission of Alamy (© Gallo Images).

Every effort has been made to contact copyright holders of material reproduced in this book. Any omissions will be rectified in subsequent printings if notice is given to the publisher.

Disclaimer
All the Internet addresses (URLs) given in this book were valid at the time of going to press. However, due to the dynamic nature of the Internet, some addresses may have changed, or sites may have changed or ceased to exist since publication. While the author and publisher regret any inconvenience this may cause readers, no responsibility for any such changes can be accepted by either the author or the publisher.

Contents

What Is Behavior? 4

Instinctive or Learned? 6

Instinct: Fight or Flight 8

Nature School 10

Mimicry 14

Do Animals Think? 16

Animal Emotions: Real or Imagined? 18

Communication 20

Courtship and Competition 22

Living Together 24

Case Study: The Chimpanzees of Gombe 26

Tool Use 30

Hug a Tree 32

Pets and Farm Animals 34

How Do I Behave? 38

Animal Behavior Timeline 42

Glossary 44

Find Out More 46

Index 48

Some words appear in the text in bold, **like this**. You can find out what they mean by looking in the glossary.

What Is Behavior?

Behavior is the way a living thing acts, or behaves. Scientists study behavior. It helps them understand more about living things like plants and animals.

Scientist Nikolaas Tinbergen created the four questions below about behavior. By asking these questions, we can better understand why a living thing behaves a certain way.

Cause	What is the **stimulus** that causes the behavior? (A stimulus, such as heat, causes a living thing to respond.)
Development	What early experiences cause the behavior to appear? How does the behavior change with age?
Evolution	How does the behavior of one **species** compare with that of a similar species? (A species is a group of living things that are able to have young together.) How might it have **evolved** (changed over time)?
Function	How does the behavior influence the animal's chance of survival? How does it affect its ability to **reproduce** (have young)?

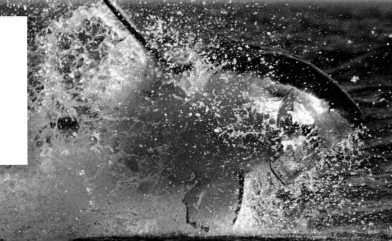

When a great white shark chases seals, it is showing a feeding behavior.

Why do you eat?

You have probably not thought too much about why you eat. But it is a behavior we all do every day. So, let's ask Tinbergen's questions about our own feeding behaviors.

Cause	What stimulus causes you to eat? Do you eat because it is time for a meal? Do you eat because you are hungry? Or do you eat because something smells good?
Development	How did you eat just after you were born? How have your eating habits changed as you have grown older?
Evolution	Millions of years ago, humans and chimpanzees developed, or evolved, from the same **ancestor** (relative from long ago). Does the way we eat show that humans and chimpanzees are related?
Function	How do you think eating allows you to survive?

Human feeding behaviors can follow a fixed pattern. For example, you might always eat the same foods at the same time of day.

Instinctive or Learned?

Behavior can be broadly divided into two types.

Instinct

Some behavior is **instinctive**. This means it comes naturally. For example, when sea turtle hatchlings come out of their nests in the sand, they head toward the sea. Scientist think they respond to the **stimulus** of the bright sky over the sea. They have not had time to learn this behavior. Rather, it comes naturally.

Learning

Other behavior is learned. It can be learned from parents. It can also be learned from an animal's own experience. An animal can change this behavior—for example, if one way of hunting works best.

Sea turtle hatchlings head instinctively in the direction of the sea.

Which way?

Each year, birds called starlings **migrate** (travel) across Europe. One year, scientists caught starlings and moved them off their usual path. When released, all the younger birds continued southwest, as before. But since they were off their usual path, this did not lead them to their usual winter home. In contrast, the older birds knew to change direction. They found their way home. But why?

Even young birds know to fly in a specific direction, such as southwest. It is an instinctive behavior. But experience teaches them to make adjustments. This is a learned behavior. So, migrating involves both instinctive and learned behaviors.

Migrating starlings usually rest in The Netherlands. But scientists moved them to Switzerland instead. See how the young starlings (red lines) got off track after this, going southwest. But the adults (blue lines) adjusted their course. They found their winter home (the white area).

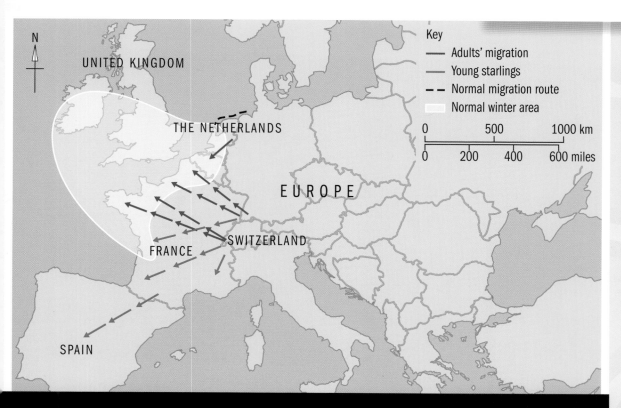

N

UNITED KINGDOM

THE NETHERLANDS

EUROPE

SWITZERLAND

FRANCE

SPAIN

Key
— Adults' migration
— Young starlings
-- Normal migration route
▢ Normal winter area

| 0 | | 500 | | 1000 km |

| 0 | 200 | 400 | 600 miles |

WORD BANK
instinctive behavior that comes naturally, without having to think about it
migrate take a two-way journey, often between winter feeding and summer
breeding sites (places where animals come together to have young)

Instinct: Fight or Flight

To survive attacks, animals have **automatic** responses. They respond without even thinking about it. They will either fight or **flee** (run away).

Red alert

If a house cat is suddenly faced with a dog, the cat's heartbeat speeds up rapidly. This pumps blood to its muscles. Its hair stands on end. This make it look bigger. All its senses are on "red-alert." The cat's body is automatically ready to fight or flee.

If a zebra is faced with a lion, it starts running for its life. But if cornered, the zebra fights. It kicks at the lion with its powerful hind legs and sharp hooves.

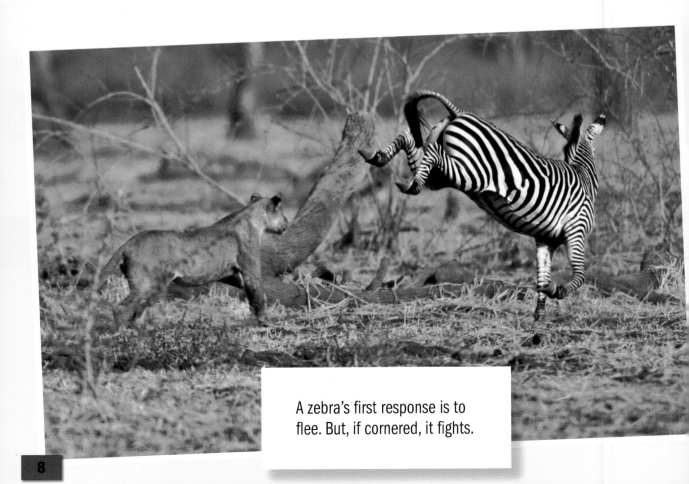

A zebra's first response is to flee. But, if cornered, it fights.

What's the message?

If a springbok spots a **predator** (animal that could eat it), it leaps straight up into the air, with stiff legs. But why?

The springbok could be warning other springboks about the predator. Or it could be attracting the predator to itself, to save the rest of the group. If several springbok leap, this is maybe meant to confuse the predator. The springbok could be also showing that it is healthy and cannot be caught. Whatever the reason, this **behavior** seems to work. The predator usually stops hunting the leaping springbok.

The springbok's stiff-legged leaping sends a message to its predators.

WORD BANK

automatic   happening without a person or animal needing to think about it

predator   animal that catches other animals for food

Nature School

Scientists have found many different learned **behaviors** among animals.

Walk time!

Pet dogs often run to the front door as soon as their owners pick up a leash. This is a result of **conditioning**. The dog learns to connect the leash with going for a walk. This behavior then becomes **automatic**.

These prairie dogs live near trails used by people. They have learned not to give alarm calls every time people walk past. They are **habituated** to people, meaning they are used to them.

Winter store

A jay bird will bury acorns in the forest in the fall. It returns to the same place to find them in winter. This is called **spatial learning**. The jay remembers the landmarks close to where it buried the acorns.

Yuck!

When a toad catches a millipede, it spits it out. This is because the millipede is covered in bad-tasting poisons. The toad quickly learns that the millipede is not good to eat. This is called **trial-and-error learning**.

Any **predator** that tries to eat a bombardier beetle learns that these beetles shoot out boiling-hot poisons. This is trial-and-error learning.

WORD BANK
conditioning process in which an animal learns to connect a certain behavior with a regular event
habituate get used to something

Monkeys that wash potatoes

Sometimes animals invent new **behaviors**. Other animals can then copy these behaviors. This happened with a group of monkeys called macaques in Japan.

Researchers placed sweet potatoes on a sandy beach near the macaques. A young female macaque named Imo learned to wash sand off the potatoes in a nearby stream. Many other monkeys **imitated** (copied) this behavior.

Imo then learned that a sweet potato tasted better when washed in seawater. Soon, most of the other young macaques copied her example. As they got older, they taught this behavior to their babies.

But few of the (mostly male) adults copied Imo. Why? The older males usually stayed apart from Imo and the other young monkeys. They did not watch and copy the behavior.

Japanese macaques learned to wash sand off sweet potatoes.

WHAT IT MEANS FOR US

By watching these macaques, scientists saw a new behavior pass through a **population** (group of animals in an area). It not only passed through the group. It also passed from one generation (age group) to the next.

Imo and the wheat grain

Researchers also put wheat grains in the sand. Imo picked up a handful of wheat and sand and threw it in the water. She learned that the sand would sink, but the wheat would float. This wheat would then be clean to eat. But Imo was unusually smart. It took the other monkeys longer to copy this behavior.

Japanese macaques have learned that hot springs keep them warm in winter.

WORD BANK
imitate   copy the behavior of others
population   group of people or animals living in an area

Mimicry

Mimicry is when one animal is so similar to another that it might be mistaken for it. Animals can **mimic** (copy) looks as well as **behavior**.

The mimic octopus

Many **species** of octopus are able to match the color of their surroundings. They do this to avoid being seen by **predators**.

The mimic octopus also mimics sea creatures that will scare off the predator. To mimic a poisonous sole fish, the mimic octopus pulls in its arms and flattens its body. It makes wavy movements. The octopus mimics the poisonous lionfish by floating just above the seabed, with its arms spread wide.

The mimic octopus above blends in with the sea floor. The octopus on the right is mimicking a poisonous sole fish.

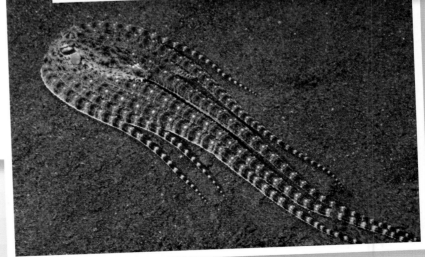

When attacked by a damselfish, the mimic octopus makes itself look like a banded sea snake—an animal that eats damselfish. The octopus turns black and yellow. It holds six of its arms against its body, waving the other two back and forth.

The male big dipper firefly is tricked to his death by females of another species.

Fatal fireflies

Some female fireflies mimic the lights of female fireflies of another species. These lights attract males of the other species. The mimicking female then captures and eats the male firefly! She gets an easy meal. She also takes in special substances that protect her from spiders.

WORD BANK
mimicry   when one animal is so similar to another that it may be mistaken for it
mimic   act or look like another animal

Do Animals Think?

People often wonder if animals have thoughts. Or are all their actions **instinctive**? Animals actually show many signs of intelligent **behavior**.

Mirror test

When you look in a mirror, you know you are seeing yourself. Researchers have used mirrors to test if animals are similarly aware of themselves. They put two black dots on an animal's face. If it looks at itself in the mirror and tries to remove the spots, this shows it knows it is seeing itself in the mirror.

At first, only the great apes—like gorillas, chimpanzees, and orangutans—passed this test. But as more animals were tested, more appeared to recognize "self." They included rhesus macaques (a kind of monkey), bottlenose dolphins, orcas (killer whales), and elephants.

Some animals recognize themselves when they look in a mirror.

Clever bird

Scientists studied a crow named Betty. They placed food in a bucket at the bottom of a tube. Could Betty think of a way to get at the food? Betty took a straight piece of wire and bent it into a hook shape. Then she lowered it into the tube. She pulled up the bucket with her hook and ate the food!

Betty could not have learned this behavior from other birds. She was being creative. This showed an unexpected level of intelligent behavior.

Betty the crow made a hook to pull a bucket of food up a tube.

Animal Emotions: Real or Imagined?

When a baby gorilla dies, the mother will carry the body for several days. Is she **mourning** (showing sadness)? If elephants see a dead elephant, they gently touch the body with their feet. What are they thinking? We know that some non-human animals experience fear and pain. But can they have **emotions** (feelings) in a similar way to humans?

These elephants are responding to the remains of another elephant.

Moody dogs

In a study of dogs, if a bowl was placed on one side of a room, it contained a treat. If it was placed on the other side, it had nothing. The dogs quickly learned which side meant a treat.

But then the bowl was placed in new positions. Some dogs ran to check the bowl. These were the **optimists**. They expected the best to happen. Others were less interested. They were the **pessimists**. They expected the worst. So, just as with people, dogs can be either optimists or pessimists.

This bloodhound might look sad. But there is a good chance it is actually an optimist!

Life experience

Animals' emotions are shaped by their everyday lives. An animal that is regularly threatened by **predators** might become a pessimist. It thinks that each noise in the grass is a predator. An animal that can easily get food is probably an optimist. It views a noise in the grass as potential **prey**, or an animal to be eaten.

WORD BANK
optimist   someone who usually expects the best to happen in any situation
pessimist   someone who usually expects the worst to happen in any situation

Communication

Animals **communicate**, or send messages to each other, in many ways. Birds and whales sing. Frogs croak. Fiddler crabs wave their claws. Squids change the color patterns on their skin. Honeybees dance.

Animals communicate for different reasons. They attract partners. They declare that a **territory** (living space) is taken. They warn of danger.

False danger warning

Animals of the same **species** often communicate with each other. But sometimes there can be communication between members of different species. In India, chital deer live with hanuman langurs. The langurs living high up in the trees spot tigers approaching. They give an alarm call to warn the deer. The deer pick up on sounds and smells of hidden tigers. They warn the langurs. In this way, two species communicate and help each other.

This shows chital deer living alongside hanuman langurs.

Body language

Animals can communicate with **body language**. When a dog wags its tail, it is happy. When a cat arches its back, it is showing **aggression** (threatening **behavior**). When an elephant sticks out it ears, it is very angry.

WHAT IT MEANS FOR US

Gray reef sharks use body language to warn other sharks —and even people—to keep away. They arch their backs and point the fins behind their head downward. They raise their snouts (noses) and swim stiffly. Anybody who fails to notice the warning is attacked.

WORD BANK
communicate send messages to each other
body language movements of the body that can communicate an animal's or person's feelings

Courtship and Competition

Many animals live alone and avoid others of their own **species**. But animals need to come together to **mate** (have young). So, some animals find creative ways to **court**, or gain the attention of, a partner.

Competition between males

Some males have to fight for the right to mate with a female. Among the red deer, the strongest stags (males) have roaring competitions. If they still seem equal, they walk alongside each other, to size each other up. If one stag does not back down, they fight. They lock antlers and push and pull, until one defeats the other. The winner has access to several female deer.

Red deer fight for the right to mate.

Female choice

Female animals often choose the strongest males. This means their **offspring** (babies) will be strong and healthy, too. So, males need to impress females.

The male bowerbird of Australia builds a nest of twigs, known as a **bower**. He decorates it with any blue objects he can find. When a female appears, the male bowerbird dances in front of his bower. If the female is impressed, she will mate with him.

Will the blue objects this male bowerbird has gathered be enough to attract a female?

WORD BANK
mate   come together to have young
offspring   babies or young

Living Together

Some animals live together in groups. They are known as **social** animals. In order to live together peacefully, social animals **communicate** and have rules.

Pecking order

In many social animal groups, each individual has its place. In wolf groups, the parents lead the pack. Their **offspring** make up the rest of the pack. The younger wolves are **submissive** to their parents, meaning they do not challenge them. If they were not submissive, then fights would break out. Fights could cause serious injury— or even death.

Wolf body language

Wolves use **body language** to show which wolves are **assertive** (confident) and which are **passive** (willing to follow others). An assertive wolf stands tall, with its tail straight out. More passive wolves walk low to the ground, with ears and tail turned down. They may lick the assertive wolf's face.

A wolf lies down on the ground. It is being submissive to an assertive wolf, probably a parent.

Cooperative hunting

Generally the wolf pack hunts as a team. They like to keep the **prey** running until it is too weak to put up a fight. Working together, they can run down prey as big as moose and deer.

By working together, wolves can bring down prey much larger than themselves.

WHAT IT MEANS FOR US

When pet dogs are left outside, they sometimes become **feral** (wild) to survive outdoors. Feral dogs form packs, like wolves. They sometimes even attack people. Since they once lived with people, they are not afraid of them.

WORD BANK
social   living with and interacting with others
submissive   giving in to the will of another

The Chimpanzees of Gombe

In 1960 scientist Jane Goodall started to research the **behavior** of chimpanzees in Gombe Stream National Park. This is in Tanzania, Africa. When she first arrived, Goodall followed the group everywhere. By seeing her every day, the chimpanzees became **habituated** to, or used to, her.

Jane Goodall's work with chimpanzees was in Gombe, Tanzania.

New discoveries

Goodall made some remarkable discoveries. First, she saw the chimpanzees eat meat and hunt other animals. Until then, chimpanzees were thought to be **vegetarians** (plant-eaters). She also found that chimpanzees use grass stems to "fish" for termites in termite mounds. Until then, scientists thought that only humans were toolmakers.

Toolmakers

Goodall noticed that when "fishing" for termites, young male and female chimpanzees behave differently. Young females learn earlier and do it more often. Males play more. Why?

When the youngsters grow up, female chimpanzees will have no time to hunt for meat as they care for babies. They will need termite-fishing skills. But adult males are expected to hunt for meat. They can play more when they are young. Their play is developing fighting and hunting skills.

This chimpanzee is "fishing" for termites.

Call	Emotion
"Wraa"	Fear
"Huu"	Confused
Food grunt or food "aaa" call	Enjoying food
Crying or whimpering	Upset
Arrival pant-hoot	Excitement

Chimp-talk

Chimpanzees **communicate** in a variety of ways, including **body language**. They also call with screams, barks, grunts, and hoots. The box at left list the **emotions** expressed by their calls.

WORD BANK
vegetarian person or animal that eats only plant food

27

Making faces

Chimpanzees have many facial expressions. When the teeth show and the lips are pulled back (right), it is an angry face. The pout face (below) is **submissive**. The play face (below right) shows that all is calm.

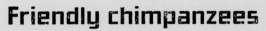

Friendly chimpanzees

Chimpanzees generally get along well. They laugh at playtime and groom (clean and brush) one another. They touch hands and enjoy tickling. Close bonds develop between family members and group members. These bonds last an entire lifetime.

A dangerous side

But there is a more dangerous side to chimpanzees. When chimpanzees go hunting, they are well organized. They work in teams, with each chimp having a clear role. The hunted animal is torn apart and shared.

Chimpanzees are often at war with their neighbors. Groups of chimpanzees will gang up on neighboring groups and kill them.

The work continues

The work that Jane Goodall started continues at the Gombe Stream Research Center. You can read more about this work at www.janegoodall.org.

Jane Goodall is shown here with a Gombe chimpanzee.

Tool Use

A surprising number of animals—and even insects—use tools.

Heron fishing

Green herons are a kind of bird. When they go fishing, they carefully place insects, feathers, and thin twigs on the water. This **baiting behavior** attracts fish up to the surface. The herons can then catch the fish more easily.

Dolphin protection

A female bottlenose dolphin in Western Australia put a sponge from the seabed over her beak. This prevented stonefish from stinging her as she searched the seabed for fish. Other dolphins copied this **foraging** (food-searching) behavior.

Dolphins use sponges to protect their beaks from dangerous fish.

Crows use traffic lights

In Japan, carrion crows use traffic lights as tools. When the traffic lights turn red, the crows place walnuts on to the road. They fly away when the lights turn green. The cars and trucks run over the walnuts and crack them open. When the lights turn red again, the crows pick up the crushed nuts.

Tool-bug

The Costa Rican assassin bug captures a worker termite from a termite nest. It sucks out all the termite's body juices. It then takes the termite's **exoskeleton** (dried skin) and hangs it over the nest. A worker termite comes to clear away the body. But the assassin bug grabs the worker termite. It has used the exoskeleton as a tool to gain another meal.

The Japanese crow (on the wire) waits for vehicles to crack the walnuts it drops in the road.

Hug a Tree

Some plant **behavior** is easy to see. For example, plants grow toward or away from sunlight. But plants can also show more surprising behaviors.

Danger: Thorn attack

In the southern United States, there is a vine-like plant called the Schrankia. When disturbed, its leaves fold up rapidly. The sudden movement scares away small plant-eaters, such as insects. The Schrankia becomes unappealing to larger animals, too. The folded-up leaves reveal sharp, dangerous thorns on the plant's stems.

Leaves of the Schrankia vine fold up to reveal sharp thorns.

Flytrap

The leaves of the Venus' flytrap plant close if a fly touches the tiny hairs on their surface. The movement of the trapped insect then causes the plant to produce substances that **digest** (break down) the fly as food. This allows the plant to live in areas without many usual food sources.

Plant talk

In the state of California, researchers clipped the leaves of sagebrush plants. This **mimicked** insect damage. The sagebrush sent out a substance that floated through the air. This was picked up by tobacco plants nearby. The tobacco plants responded by producing substances that made their leaves taste bad. This ensured that insects would not eat them, too. The research proves that one plant can **communicate** with another.

WORD BANK
digest break down and process food

Pets and Farm Animals

Many animals have learned to live as pets and farm animals. For example, the **ancestors** of the dogs we have as pets are gray wolves (see pages 24 and 25). Over time, they became **domesticated**, meaning they learned to live alongside people.

Puppy love

Puppies show the same **behaviors** as wolf cubs. Young pups have play fights. These teach them to deal with other dogs. Their mother disciplines them by staring at them, just as mother wolves do. She scolds them with growls. Puppies sometimes beg for food from an adult dog by licking its face. The adult might **regurgitate** (throw up) food, just as wolves do. It is an **instinctive** behavior.

Life in the home

A dog might consider its owners to be similar to pack leaders, or parent wolves. Dogs will roll onto their back, exposing their stomach. They might also nuzzle or lick an owner's face. This is the way a **passive** wolf behaves around a more **assertive**—possibly parent—wolf.

When tired, a dog might scrape the carpet and circle the spot before lying down. Wolves use the same behavior to prepare a place on the ground for the night.

Common confusions

Smiling dogs

An angry dog pulls back its lips to expose its teeth. This looks as if it is smiling. But this is not like a human smile. It is showing **aggression** and might attack. This **body language** can be traced back to dogs' ancestor, the wolf.

When a dog licks your face, this is similar to wolf behavior.

WORD BANK
domesticated tamed to live alongside people
regurgitate bring up or throw up food from the stomach

Animal welfare

By understanding the **behavior** of wild animals, scientists are learning how to make the lives of pets and farm animals more comfortable.

Some animals need to act out natural behaviors. For example, some animals need to show **foraging** behaviors. Pigs need to root around, pushing their snouts into the earth—even if a farmer feeds them well. Since foraging makes pigs happy, many people argue they should be allowed to do it.

Battery cages

Chickens raised for food are sometimes kept in small indoor cages called **battery cages**. Chickens are happier when they have space to roam, scratch, and peck. They also seem happier when they build nests. So, battery cages work against the chickens' **instinctive** behaviors. For this reason, many people think battery cages are cruel.

Egg-laying chickens are crammed into a battery cage on a farm. They remain there for an entire year before being killed.

Very comfortable, thank you!

Wild sows (female pigs) that are about to give birth build nests out of dried plants. But farm sows that are given large water beds are happy to give birth on the water bed instead. The comfort of the nest is more important to them than the nest-building behavior.

Clearly, some kinds of behaviors are more important to animals than others. These kinds of discoveries help us give animals the best possible care.

Pigs need some sort of nest before having babies.

WORD BANK

battery cage type of small indoor cage used to raise many chickens very cheaply

How Do I Behave?

Humans behave in many interesting ways. Let's look at some of the more basic forms of human **behavior**.

Instinct

Like other animals, humans show **instinctive** behaviors. Quickly pulling back our hand if we touch a hot saucepan is a behavioral **reflex**. A reflex is a reaction that happens **automatically**. It is one of the simplest forms of human behavior.

Hanging on

When a newborn baby grasps a finger and is lifted up, it instinctively holds on tight. This probably dates back to our primate ancestors. Most primates are always on the move to find food. So, babies automatically hold their mother's fur. This way, they do not fall off when she moves.

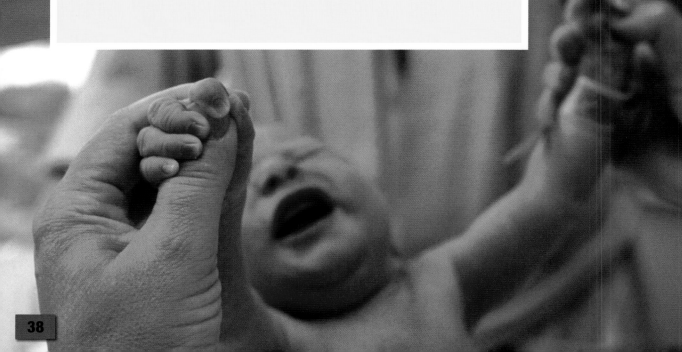

Common confusions

Body language

Humans **communicate** with **body language** (see page 21) . But these signals can sometimes be confusing. In the United States, people who maintain eye contact are considered confident. Those who look away constantly are thought to be less comfortable. But in parts of Asia, looking somebody in the eye is considered rude.

Living together

Humans are **social** animals. We band together as families, friends, and nations (countries). This probably dates back to our **primate ancestors** millions of years ago. (Primates are a group of animals that include monkeys and apes.) They formed hunting groups to kill more animals for food.

Past, present, and future

Millions of years ago, our **ancestors** did not plan for the future. The did not remember the past. But since modern humans have **evolved**, we can **communicate** about the past and future. It is one thing that makes humans unique.

Mysterious behavior

Yet scientists are still trying to understand some of our most basic everyday **behaviors**.

Blushing

When we blush (turn red or pink in the face), it gives away the fact the we feel uncomfortable. No one knows why we do it.

Laughter

Why do we laugh? It could be because laughing causes our bodies to produce mood-improving substances called **endorphins**. Laughter could also be a **social** behavior. It strengthens the relationships between people.

Laughing helps people to bond with each other.

Teenagers

Most animals, including the great apes, move quickly from being babies to being adults. But humans spend a long time as teenagers. Why is this? Scientists think the brain gets reorganized during the teenage years. This reorganization probably allows the mind to handle social situations. This makes us different from all other animals.

Art

Another human mystery is art. Why do we create images of things around us? Perhaps it was once a way to impress a partner. Or it could have been a "social glue" that bonded our ancestors to their families and groups.

Body language is an important kind of human behavior.

Animal Behavior Timeline

2,200 years ago Greek thinker Aristotle writes about animal **behavior**.

1775 Beekeeper Johann Ernst Spitzner writes about dancing in bees.

1861 Henry Walter Bates writes about **mimicry** in animals.

1872 Charles Darwin describes the outward signs of **emotions** in people. He also shows that these signs are similar to signs in animals.

1872 Douglas Spalding studies the behavior of chickens. He notes that young chicks will quickly become attached to the first thing they see after they hatch, seeing it as a "mother." This is called **imprinting**.

1901 Ivan Pavlov studies the behavior of dogs. He learns about their **instinctive** behaviors.

1923 Karl Ritter von Frisch writes about the way bees **communicate**.

1935 Konrad Lorenz writes about imprinting in geese.

1944 Donald Griffin and Robert Galambos study the behavior of bats. Griffin goes on to study "animal thinking."

1951 Nikolaas Tinbergen examines instinctive behaviors.

1953 Kinji Imanishi and Syunzo Kawamura study Japanese monkeys called macaques (see pages 12 and 13). They notice how monkeys can learn behaviors by copying other monkeys.

1965 Jane Goodall writes about the Gombe chimpanzee (see pages 26 to 29).

1968 Nikolaas Tinbergen works with filmmaker Hugh Falkus on a movie called *Signals of Survival.* It is one of the first movies to study animal behavior.

1970 Gordon G. Gallup, Jr., develops the "mirror test" (see page 16). This shows whether animals are self-aware. He discovers that chimpanzees can recognize themselves in a mirror.

1979 Francine "Penny" Patterson teaches a version of American sign language for the deaf to two gorillas.

1983 Dian Fossey writes *Gorillas in the Mist*. It is about her study of mountain gorilla behavior in Rwanda, Africa.

1990 Filmmaker David Attenborough presents *The Trials of Life*. This movie explores animal behavior and the journeys of animals from birth to death.

2002 Alex Kacelnik reveals that a crow named Betty is able to make and use tools out of pieces of metal (see page 17).

Glossary

aggression intending or threatening to cause harm to a member of the same or another species

ancestor relative from long ago

assertive bold or confident

automatic happening without a person or animal needing to think about it

baiting using food to attract animals to come closer or to catch them

battery cage type of small indoor cage used to raise many chickens very cheaply. Sixty percent of the world's eggs are produced this way.

behavior way a living thing acts

body language movements of the body that can communicate an animal's or person's feelings

bower large nest made of twigs, grass, and bright objects by the bowerbird

communicate send messages to each other

conditioning process in which an animal learns to connect a certain behavior with a regular event

court attempt to gain the attention of a partner

digest break down and process food

domesticated tamed to live alongside people

emotion feeling

endorphin mood-improving substance created by the body

evolve develop gradually over time. This leads to evolution, which is the gradual change of characteristics of a group of living things from one generation to the next.

exoskeleton hard outer "skin" of insects, spiders, crabs, and lobsters

feral wild. Domesticated animals or pets may go back to living as feral animals.

flee run away

foraging searching for food

habituate get used to something

imitate copy the behavior of others

imprinting learning behavior in which young chicks quickly become attached to the first thing they see after they hatch, seeing it as a "mother"

instinctive behavior that comes naturally, without having to think about it

mate come together to have young

migrate take a two-way journey, often between winter feeding and summer breeding sites (places where animals come together to try to have young)

mimic act or look like another animal

mimicry when one animal is so similar to another that it may be mistaken for it

mourn express sadness over the dead

offspring babies or young

optimist someone who usually expects the best to happen in any situation

passive inactive or willing to follow others

pessimist someone who usually expects the worst to happen in any situation

population group of people or animals living in an area

predator animal that catches other animals for food

prey animal that is caught for food

primate member of a group of mammals with grasping hands and feet, nails, a short snout, eyes facing forward, and a large brain

reflex reaction that happens automatically

regurgitate bring up or throw up food from the stomach

reproduce have young

social living with and interacting with others

spatial learning learning to remember a location based on certain landmarks

species group of similar living things that are able to have young with each other

stimulus something that causes a living thing to respond

submissive giving in to the will of another

territory living space defended by an animal or group of animals

trial-and-error learning learning to do—or not do—something based on past successes and failures

vegetarian person or animal that eats only plant food

Find Out More

Books

Animals: A Children's Encyclopedia. New York: Dorling Kindersley, 2008.

Bright, Michael. *The Diversity of Species* (Timeline: Life on Earth). Chicago: Heinemann Library, 2009.

Bright, Michael. *Extinctions of Living Things* (Timeline: Life on Earth). Chicago: Heinemann Library, 2009.

Burnie, David. *How Animals Work.* New York: Dorling Kindersley, 2010.

Johnson, Jinny. *Animal Tracks and Signs.* Washington, D.C.: National Geographic, 2008.

Websites

www.nationalgeographic.com
National Geographic's website provides more information about wildlife and animal behavior.

www.amnh.org
Explore the natural world on the American Museum of Natural History's website.

http://kids.discovery.com/tell-me/animals
The Discovery Kids website has lots of information about all kinds of animals.

www.arkive.org
Arkive is a website with information, photos, and video images exploring the world's endangered species (animals in danger of dying out).

www.seaworld.org/animal-info/animal-bytes
Check out Sea World's "Animal Bytes" section of its website to find more information about selected animals.

http://animal.discovery.com
The Animal Planet website has lots of information about the behavior of wild animals and pets.

http://users.ox.ac.uk/~kgroup/tools/introduction.shtml
Learn more about research into Betty the crow.

DVDs/Blue-ray

Life (BBC/Warner Brothers, 2010)
This series is about the intelligent and sometimes amazing ways animals and plants survive.

Understanding Animal Behavior (Show Me Science) (TMW Media Group, 2008) The movie examines animal behavior. It was made specifically for students.

Topics to research

Communication

See what you can find out about people trying to communicate directly with animals. Researchers have used human sign languages and the English language itself. They have also used other things, such as computers, touch screens, and different-shaped objects. There have been experiments with gorillas, chimpanzees, parrots, and dolphins. Which animals do you think respond best to these experiments? What do you think it tells us about their intelligence? Look out for Koko, Tanzi, and Alex.

Echolocation

Investigate echolocation behavior. Echolocation is an animal's ability to find something based on the timing of echoes. Which animals echolocate to find their way around, and how do they do it? You have maybe heard about echolocation in bats, dolphins, and killer whales. But what about fruit bats, seals, and shrews,? Explore the names James Holman, Daniel Kish, Ben Underwood, and Lawrence Scadden and see what you find out.

Index

aggression 21, 35
alarm calls and signals 10, 20
animal welfare 36–37
art 41
assassin bugs 31

babies, human 38, 41
behavior
  causes 4, 5
  development 4, 5
  evolution 4, 5, 40
  function 4, 5
  instinctive 6, 7, 8–9, 34, 38
  learned 6, 7, 10–13
  modification 4, 6
birds 7, 11, 17, 20, 23, 30
blushing 40
body language 21, 24, 27, 35, 39, 41
bowerbirds 23

cats 8, 21
chickens 36, 42
chimpanzees 5, 16, 26–29, 42, 43, 47
communication 20–21, 27, 33, 39, 40, 42, 47
competition 22
conditioning 10
cooperative behavior 25
courtship 22–23
crows 7, 31, 43

deer 20, 22
dogs 8, 10, 19, 21, 25, 34–35, 42
dolphins 16, 30, 47
dominant animals 24, 28, 34

echolocation 47
elephants 16, 18, 21
emotional capacity 18–19, 27, 42
evolution 4, 5, 40

facial expressions 28, 35, 39
feeding behavior 4, 5, 12, 13, 17, 26, 27, 30, 31
fight or flight 8–9
fireflies 15
foraging 30, 36

gorillas 16, 18, 43, 47
great apes 16, 41

habituation 10, 26
herons 30
human behavior 5, 16, 38–41
hunting 6, 9, 25, 26, 27, 39

imitation 12
instinctive behavior 6, 7, 16, 34, 36, 38, 42
intelligent behavior 16–17
invention 12, 17

laughter 40, 42
learned behavior 6, 7, 10–13, 17, 19, 27, 34

macaques 12–13, 16, 42
migration 7
mimicry 14–15, 33, 42
monkeys 12–13, 16, 42

nest building 23, 36, 37

octopuses 14–15
optimists and pessimists 19

pecking orders 24
pigs 36, 37
plant behavior 32–33
play 27, 28, 34
prairie dogs 10
predators 9, 11, 14, 19
primates 38, 39

reflex actions 4, 38

self-awareness 16, 43
sharks 4, 21
social animals 24–25, 39
spatial learning 11
spiders 15
springboks 9
stimulus 4, 5, 6
submissive behavior 24, 28,

teenagers 41
tool use 17, 26, 27, 30–31
trial-and-error learning 11
turtles 6

Venus flytrap 33

wolves 24–25, 34–35